ROSEMC

THE RHS BLOOMS I

GW00384808

Lady Anne Berry VMH (Lady Anne Pal.
Rosemoor in 1959. When she gave it, as well as her house and 13ha
(32 acres) of land, to the RHS in 1988, it had matured into a fine
garden with fine collections of many rare and
interesting plants.

The RHS decided to make Rosemoor its
centre in the West Country as a focal point
there for the Society's activities. Subsequently the garden has been expanded across
most of the grassland to combine the
Society's aims of demonstrating horticul-
tural excellence with the creation of a place of beauty and pleasure for
visitors. The Robin Herbert Centre is now a place of frequent activity
with lectures, workshops and meetings combining both education
and social enjoyment.

Planting the new Rosemoor has been an exhilarating challenge.
I hope you will enjoy it and benefit from the demonstrations and
come back again to witness a great national garden maturing.

Sir Simon Hornby
PRESIDENT, RHS

Opposite: The Bog Garden, viewed from the bridge, displays a wide range of moisture-
loving plants, here *Astilbe* 'Montgomery' in bloom

Cover: The authentically constructed thatched summerhouse in the Cottage Garden

◀ **See Garden Plan, left (under flap)**

1 Robin Herbert Centre	11 Bog Garden and Lake
2 Modern Rose Garden	12 Fruit and Vegetable Garden
2a Model Gardens	13 Underpass Track
3 Shrub Rose Garden	14 Main Lawn
4 Spiral Garden	15 Old Car Park
4a Winter Garden	16 Rosemoor House
5 Square Garden	17 Old Kitchen Garden
6 Long Border	18 Woodland Garden
7 Herb Garden, Potager, Cottage Garden	19 Stone Garden
8 Foliage and Plantsman's Gardens	20 Old Tennis Court
9 Stream Garden Field	21 Croquet Lawn
10 Stream Garden	22 Arboretum

INTRODUCTION

Nestling in the wooded valley of the River Torridge, Rosemoor is a delightful garden, in an unusually beautiful setting. Here a wide range of garden styles are displayed: side by side are the very personal garden created by Lady Anne Berry VMH and the new garden area containing many interesting and attractive features, the latter continually being added to in accordance with the Society's plans for the development of Rosemoor Garden.

Rosemoor was given to The Royal Horticultural Society by Lady Anne Berry in 1988, together with the rest of the Rosemoor Estate, amounting in total to some 16ha (40 acres). The Estate had been owned by Lady Anne's family since 1923, and the house was originally used as a fishing lodge. Rosemoor was the Society's first Regional Garden and incorporates a

Common oak and ash frame golden *Robinia pseudoacacia* 'Frisia' and Rosemoor House across the Main Lawn

2

Regional Centre. As such its principal purpose is to serve RHS members (and widen membership) in the south-west, and to provide facilities for affiliated organisations.

The garden lies 1.6km (one mile) south of the town of Great Torrington, on the west-facing slopes of the Torridge valley, at around 30m (98½ft) above sea level, and enclosed on all sides by woodland. The soil is a moderately acid, heavy, silty clay loam, with a pH of around 5.5. Rainfall averages 1010mm (40in) per year, and while the climate might overall be described as fairly mild, the valley bottom site is a frost pocket, and sharp frosts with a temperature of −9°C (16°F) or below may occur in winter. Damage from late spring frosts is also a feature of the area.

Development of the original garden in the north-east corner of the estate (around Rosemoor House) began in 1959, after Lady Anne Berry met the noted plantsman Collingwood Ingram in Spain. There were already a few exotic trees growing there, for example a fine Turkey oak (*Quercus cerris*) in the Main Lawn, and two tulip trees (*Liriodendron tulipifera*) near the house. But virtually the whole of the garden around Rosemoor House as it exists now has been created in the last 30 years.

View from the Terrace towards the thatched summerhouse. Verbenas, lobelias and shrubby salvias are among the tender perennial summer bedding here

Thus Rosemoor Garden breaks down into two distinct areas: the original garden, now called Lady Anne's Garden, and the New Garden Area. The latter is effectively all of the estate apart from Lady Anne's original garden. The Garden is bisected by the B3220 road, and the two halves of the Garden, east and west, are joined by an Underpass, which emerges into Lady Anne's Garden at the southern end of the Arboretum.

This guide takes the visitor on a circular tour, beginning at the garden entrance in the Robin Herbert Centre, taking in first all of the New Garden Area and then Lady Anne's Garden.

THE ENTRANCE AND PARKLAND

On entering Rosemoor, the attractiveness of its setting is immediately obvious, with steep wooded valley slopes rising to the west beyond the River Torridge. Around the entrance and car park, and in the parkland to the south, are planted groups of forest trees in a range of genera including *Tilia* (lime), *Fraxinus* (ash), *Fagus* and *Nothofagus* (beech and southern beech), and *Quercus* (oak). On either side of the entrance two groups of the weeping silver lime (*Tilia petiolaris*), will rapidly form an imposing feature.

Above: Many of the plants along the warm west-facing wall below the Terrace are from the Southern Hemisphere. *Yucca gloriosa* 'Variegata', *Euphorbia characias* and yellow *Cytisus* 'Porlock' make a striking combination of form, colour and foliage

THE ROBIN HERBERT CENTRE

The Robin Herbert Centre, named for the Society's President at the time Rosemoor was acquired by the RHS, is a pleasing building, with numerous facilities for visitors. The initial building phase was completed in spring 1990, and the last phase, the Lecture Wing, followed in 1994. The Restaurant is in the south wing, while the north wing houses the Lecture

Theatre, where workshops and demonstrations are also held. To the right of the entrance foyer is the Shop, and immediately outside the Shop is the Plant Centre. The plants sold here reflect the range of genera grown at Rosemoor, making this the widest selection of plants available in Devon.

The Robin Herbert Centre sits upon a platform overlooking the Formal Garden to the west. The Courtyard immediately outside is bounded by the Restaurant and Lecture Theatre to the left and right respectively. To the south of the Restaurant a terrace area with raised beds for alpine plants also serves as an overflow for the Restaurant during busy periods.

A panoramic view from the Terrace. The fountain is the focal point of the four formal gardens

The Courtyard and Terrace

In the Courtyard four specimens of *Acer palmatum* 'Osakazuki' have been planted in the L-shaped beds. These will slowly grow into large spreading bushes, with attractive foliage and fine autumn colour. The Courtyard contains seasonal plantings, with tender perennials for summer display, a theme shared by the long beds alongside the ramps leading down to the Formal Garden.

The platform upon which the Robin Herbert Centre sits provides a generous stretch of west-facing wall immediately below the Terrace. Plantings here include many subjects from the Southern Hemisphere, taking advantage of the shelter of the wall, and a strong representation of climbers. Among the shrubs are several species of *Olearia* from Australia and New Zealand. Other genera from south of the equator include *Drimys, Acca (Feijoa)*, and *Pittosporum*, good evergreen subjects, which thrive in the mild and moist south-west climate.

The fountain with the Square (hot) Garden beyond. Children are welcomed at Rosemoor and encouraged to become a Rosemoor Explorer with the children's map and quiz

THE FORMAL GARDEN

Occupying the entire 3ha (7½ acres) of the square field, the Formal Garden is the most intensively cultivated area at Rosemoor. Here a range of distinctive gardens and other features have been developed within quadrants, each designed with axial paths. These gardens and borders contain a mixture of plantings for display and demonstration, designed both to please the eye and to educate the visitor.

The Terrace is raised 2.4m (8ft) above the Formal Garden, and from the top of the steps affords a fine view along the east-west axis to the wooded slopes beyond. From this point the four formal square gardens at the heart of the square field can be seen, each enclosed within hedges which will eventually reach some 2.4m (8ft) high. These also provide a backdrop for the mixed double border which runs from south to north along the 180m (200yd) width of the field.

2 3

Visitors discuss one of the more than 50 cultivars in the Modern Rose Garden

The Rose Gardens

The first two formal squares immediately below the Terrace are dedicated to roses, and were planted in spring 1990.

The Modern Rose Garden, on the left (south-west), contains over 50 cultivars. Here hybrid tea and floribunda roses predominate (recently reclassified as large- and cluster-flowered respectively), with a mixture of climbing varieties in both groups to clothe the obelisk-shaped pillars. The cultivars have been carefully chosen for resistance to disease, which can be a particular problem in the clean air and rather soft and damp growing conditions which prevail in the West Country. They are also fine and vigorous examples in the range of colours and sizes represented, scent being an important criterion for inclusion.

The Shrub Rose Garden, to the right (north-east) of the Modern Rose Garden, contrasts strongly with the more angular design of its neighbour. In the larger of the two ovals is a catenary, a number of pillars to support climbers and ramblers, a rope joining them, along which the stronger-growing cultivars are trained. The Shrub Rose Garden contains a diverse collection, 130 cultivars among the nearly 500 roses. In the two ovals older groups such as the Albas, Centifolias and Moss roses dominate, whilst in the outer beds more modern cultivars may be found. The groups represented take the story of shrub roses from its very beginnings to the

Visitors in the Modern Rose Garden

present day, with modern hybrids such as English roses demonstrating up-to-the-minute developments in breeding. To complement this collection, a wide range of other interesting shrub and species roses may be seen in Lady Anne's Garden (see p. 18). The rich scents of the majority of the shrub roses make this garden a delight for nose and eye from early to mid summer.

Colour Theme Gardens

The two lower (western) formal squares are given over to colour theme gardens. Their internal designs, as those of the rose gardens, contrast strongly.

The Spiral Garden Below (west of) the Modern Rose Garden, the Spiral Garden's path winds in towards its centre, with the shape echoed in the plantings by the hedge within the borders. The spiral ends in a paved area containing two semi-circular seats at the heart of the garden. The plantings are of soft flower colours and tones, complemented by silver and variegated foliage. Shrubs provide the backbone of the borders, whose colours flow around the garden from pale yellow and green through pale blue to mauve and violet, then pink, peach and apricot to yellow again. Towards the centre the colours gradually fade to predominantly white and grey.

The Square Garden Below (west of) the Shrub Rose Garden, the Square Garden is a complete contrast in design and colour. Hot colours predominate with a vibrant mixture of red, orange, yellow and purple. These colours contrast well with the bright foliage of the shrubs and trees which have been planted to provide structural interest in this area.

The Spiral Garden overflows with cool grey, silver and blue foliage plants

The Square (hot) Garden is designed to show successful planting in a range of fiery colours

8

The Long Border

Between the upper and lower formal squares, a double herba-ceous border runs the full width of the square field. The border has been designed to provide colour from late spring until autumn. The border is divided into discreet sections within low hedged 'walls', each of which may be seen as a self-contained border in itself, but which may also be seen as a part of the greater border from a distance. The individual borders have a strong backbone of shrub planting, with long drifts of herbaceous plants to the rear, becoming more intimate in scale towards the front.

The double Long Border. This section is replete with the intense blues and purples of salvias, delphiniums and campanulas. White irises are counter-points

The colour scheme of the first section uses flowers of mainly pink, mauve-blue, white and soft yellow, with silver, blue and purple foliage. Among the larger-growing perennials, *Thalictrum* cultivars make effective back-border subjects, with delicate glau-cous foliage, and white or yellow flowers. Another back border plant, the plume poppy, *Macleaya microcarpa* 'Kelway's Coral Plume', provides a much heavier effect with its handsome grey-green lobed leaves, overtopped by delicate airy sprays of pink. Amongst other tall-growing perennials are numerous cultivars of *Campanula* and monkshood (*Aconitum*).

In the centre and front of the borders a range of hardy gera-niums, *Hemerocallis* (daylilies), and *Anemone* cultivars provide a succession of flowers from spring through to early autumn. Among and between the perennials, summer-flowering bulbous subjects such as lilies and galtonias contribute to the overall display.

As the border leads northwards the colour mix gradually changes, the initial purple, blue and orange lessening in intensity to yellow, with pink and pale blue, and finally gradually fading to cream and white with variegated foliage as the border leads out into the Stream Garden Field.

Opposite: A young visitor enjoys lupins and other colourful flowers in the Cottage Garden

In this area of the Herb Garden an interesting selection of potted thymes creates a patchwork

Herb Garden, Potager and Cottage Garden

Immediately north of the Shrub Rose Garden is an area enclosed within a mixed beech and hornbeam hedge. This contains three distinct gardens with strong elements of planting and landscaping in common. A dry-stone wall built in a West Country style bisects the area, with the Herb Garden and Potager to the south, and the Cottage Garden to the north.

The Herb Garden has been designed to incorporate many features for the disabled. The design avoids the use of steps, despite the sloping site. The bricks used in the paths provide a good all-weather surface, and parking bays for wheelchairs have been provided. Raised beds allow many plants to be seen and appreciated more closely (as with the thyme collection growing in the large raised bed to the south-east). The plantings in the Herb Garden cover the entire range of medicinal, culinary and other herbs.

The Potager lies to the north of the Herb Garden. Its name is taken from the French term *Jardin Potager*, and it is effectively an ornamental kitchen garden. Four beds are arranged in a circle, enclosed within a number of tall wrought-iron arches, each supporting a variety of hardy grape vine. The large metal arch in the centre of the Potager has two cultivars of *Wisteria* growing over it. In the beds vegetables are arranged in groups to contrast foliage,

In the Potager grape vines cover the pergolas, while (from left) cucumber, parsley, red cabbages and runner beans thrive

form and colour, more in the manner of a herbaceous border, avoiding allotment-style rows.

The Cottage Garden takes up the area to the north of the Potager. Its principal feature is an authentically constructed thatched summerhouse, built of local oak without the use of screws or nails, and walls made of wattle and daub. Plantings in the Cottage Garden are less contrived than elsewhere in the Formal Garden, and bright and colourful flowers jostle together with far less concern for colour associations. Scent is a very important element in this garden. Occasional vegetables and fruit can also be found growing here in amongst the more decorative plantings. A small collection of local cultivars of apples are grown in the orchard which occupies the north-west corner of the area.

8

Foliage and Plantsman's Gardens

Immediately across the path to the west of the Herb Garden, another two complementary themes are combined in the Foliage and Plantsman's Gardens. Here the formality which characterises much of the design in the Formal Garden gives way to a more organic style, with flowing paths and lines. This reflects the emphasis on natural form in the Foliage Garden itself, where the contrasting shapes and colours of plant and leaf provide interest over a prolonged season. Among the groups strongly represented here are grasses and grass-like plants, from the tall slightly tender *Arundo donax*, whose glaucous stems can reach over 3 m (10ft) in a season, to low sedges (*Carex* species) a few centimetres tall. The range of leaf colours in the grasses is very wide, apart from greens and blues, it

encompasses red, brown, gold and
many types of variegation. Many
grasses, for example the oat grasses
(*Stipa* species), and the pampas
grass (*Cortaderia*), also bear attractive flowers.

Among the grasses in the Foliage
Garden are many plants with distinctive form and leaf colour.

A dry-stone planting bed for
alpines and dwarf shrubs divides
the Foliage and Plantsman's Gardens. The Plantsman's Garden has
been designed to enable the widest
range of interesting and unusual
plants to be accommodated, many
of West Country origin, in conditions ranging from woodland to
open and sunny. The plantings are
set out in broad geographical
groupings, with northern hemisphere woodland plants in the sha-
dier areas, while southern hemisphere subjects predominate
around the north entrance.

The strong forms of
grasses and architectural
plants in the Foliage
Garden are visually
intriguing

Winter and Model Gardens

To the south of the square field plantings continue in a much
less formal vein. The axis of the Long Border terminates with
a curved holly hedge. In the south-west corner the Winter
Garden demonstrates as complete a range of plants for winter
interest, including leaf, form, fruit, bark, stems and flower,
as can be grown at Rosemoor. In due course a rustic stone
shelter which faces the Visitors Centre and has its back to
the prevailing south-westerly winds will be built in this
area.

To the east of the Long Border axis three Model Gardens are
being built. These are arranged around an informal central
lawn and are intended to be distinct in their themes but
complementary to one another. Design and planning princi-
ples on a more domestic scale are intended to be demonstrated
here.

Opposite: A colourful display of waterside plants in the Stream Garden includes *Caltha palustris polypetala, Iris pseudacorus* 'Variegata', primulas, euphorbias and ostrich fern, *Matteuccia struthiopteris*

THE STREAM GARDEN FIELD

The path to Lady Anne's Garden leaves the square field through the gap in the centre of the hedge. As the track rounds the large oak to the left, a young plant of the Lucombe oak, *Quercus* × *hispanica* 'Lucombeana' can be seen, planted to mark the opening of the new garden in June 1990. The plantings in the Stream Garden Field are designed to provide a quieter interlude between the Formal Garden and the brighter plantings in the Stream and Bog Garden. Among the larger trees, the walnut family is represented by several species of true walnut (*Juglans*), and a number of hickories from North America (*Carya*). There are several major genera of flowering trees, including flowering crabs (*Malus*) in pale pink and white, and early-flowering cherries (*Prunus*). The theme of pale and pastel shades is continued in the shrubby underplantings.

The Stream Garden showing the new rockwork, looking towards the underpass leading to Lady Anne's Garden

14

THE STREAM GARDEN, BOG
GARDEN AND LAKE

A gardener planting *Iris ensata* on the edge of the Lake

The track leads down to a small bridge over a spring-fed stream. The path leading to the Underpass and Lady Anne's Garden bears to the right. Above and below the bridge, along a natural spring which flows throughout the winter, a range of marginal plantings have been developed. In the wet conditions giant perennials such as *Gunnera manicata* from Brazil, whose leafy parasols may exceed 3m (10ft) across, jostle alongside the broad metre-long leaf blades of *Lysichiton* from North America and the Far East, with bold drifts of irises, including the native yellow flag, and many ferns, particularly the ostrich fern (*Matteuccia struthiopteris*). Early colour from calthas, irises and primulas is continued by ligularias and persicarias. Throughout the season the contrast of foliage gives interest.

The Lake, built initially as a reservoir for the Garden, was subsequently planted with a wide range of marginal and aquatic plants, including water lilies. To the north and south of the Lake bold drifts of coloured-stemmed dogwoods and willows provide winter interest.

Looking due north of the bridge, the town of Torrington can be seen on a ridge above the steeply sloping common land which surrounds it on three sides. The buildings at the edge of the field were at one time part of the dairy at Rosemoor, and include a large barn known locally as a Shippon.

12

THE FRUIT AND VEGETABLE GARDEN

Opened in spring 1994, the Fruit and Vegetable Garden demonstrates techniques of growing and varieties appropriate for local conditions. To the north and east a 2.4m (8ft) high wall dressed with local stone provides sheltered conditions for many trained fruit trees. A rustic thatched arbour sits at the centre of the north wall. To the south and west split chestnut paling fencing provides a permeable boundary, allowing frost to drain away, and again providing support for trained trees.

Within the beds in the garden a wide range of techniques of growing both fruit and vegetables can be seen, with an area for container-grown subjects and a small greenhouse also. A three-course rotation for vegetables occupies the north-east corner, with the more out-of-the way subjects such as asparagus to the north-west. A small fruit cage accommodates a domestic scale planting in the centre of the north-west section.

Red onions are among the bounty at harvest time

The Fruit and Vegetable Garden is enclosed by a small orchard specialising in local top fruit varieties, particularly apples. The Fruit Garden Field has been planted with largely edible subjects, from walnuts and sweet chestnuts (*Castanea sativa* cultivars), to cob nuts (*Corylus* cultivars). Spring flower is provided by almonds (*Prunus dulcis*) and a number of crab apples (*Malus* cultivars), which also bear attractive fruits.

13

THE UNDERPASS TRACK

The Underpass joining the two halves of Rosemoor was built in 1989. The slopes have been clad with large pieces of local stone and interplanted to provide the effect of walking through a deep rocky gully.

Beyond the Underpass, a waterfall and associated rockwork continue this theme until you emerge into the Arboretum. Much of this land lends itself to growing woodland plants, particularly ferns, including several native species in the waterfall area.

The Underpass Track emerges into Lady Anne's Garden at the south end of the Arboretum. This part of the garden is very wet, and a number of alders (*Alnus* spp.), which are very tolerant of damp conditions, have been planted on the left-hand side of the path. Particularly striking is *Alnus maximowiczii*, a species with catkins 10-15cm (4-6in) long in the spring, followed by striking bold foliage.

Lady Anne's Garden is renowned for spring colour. Here the house is viewed through drifts of daffodils

The Underpass Track joins the Main Drive which effectively bisects this part of Lady Anne's Garden. To the west is a vista to Rosemoor House, with beds and borders on either side containing a diverse mixture of trees, shrubs, herbaceous plants and bulbs. Below this is an area of woodland garden around the track known as Lock's Trail, parallel to the road. This trail emerges behind Rosemoor House.

East of the Main Drive and south of the house an area of divided gardens has been developed, in many instances using existing features to provide opportunities to accommodate a wide range of plants within a comparatively small space. The Old Kitchen Garden, Stone Garden, Tennis Court, Croquet Lawn and Woodland Garden all fall within this part of the Garden. Further plantings of note are to be found around Rosemoor House itself.

Lady Anne's Garden houses a rich and varied collection of plants, many rare and unusual, with the accent particularly on trees and shrubs. A large proportion of them have been collected from the wild, many by Lady Anne herself. The botanical value of the collection is greatly enhanced by the large number of plants of known origin grown here.

14

THE MAIN LAWN

Flanked on either side by planting, the Main Lawn runs the length of the vista to Rosemoor House. Immediately to the left a large island bed of herbaceous perennials contains a range of flowering and foliage subjects, planted for year-round display. This begins in winter with *Primula vulgaris* 'Sibthorpii', followed by several lungworts (*Pulmonaria* species), the most colourful of which is the intense blue *P. angustifolia* 'Azurea'. The ferny blue-grey foliage of *Dicentra* 'Langtrees' appears in early spring, soon followed by its attractive pale mauve-pink flowers.

The heavy moist soil in this bed provides good conditions for perennials which appreciate damp conditions, such as *Trollius, Astilbe, Iris pseudacorus* 'Variegata', and hostas. A number of *Iris sibirica* cultivars also do well here, as does the exceptionally dark purple-black *I. chrysographes* 'Black Knight'.

Spring foliage of *Ligularia dentata* 'Desdemona' and *Acer palmatum* 'Atropurpureum' with irises by the Main Lawn in Lady Anne's Garden

An interesting and handsome evergreen fern, *Blechnum chilense* grows in the centre of the bed.

Continuing along the Main Lawn, the beds to the right are each planted to follow a colour theme, the first with yellow, orange and bronze flowers and purple foliage, and the second white and silver. In that bed is a fine young plant of an unusual conifer, the Japanese umbrella pine, *Sciadopitys verticillata*. An interesting range of euphorbias also grow here, including the herbaceous species *E. palustris*, with long-lasting bold heads of yellow bracts, followed by fine pinky-orange autumn colour.

Immediately across the road from Rosemoor House is a rare conifer from New Zealand, *Podocarpus acutifolius*, with yellow-green foliage which in winter turns an attractive bronzy gold. The beds to the front of the house contain a number of interesting tender plants, grown here to take advantage of the sheltered microclimate. From Rosemoor House the road then leads on towards the Old Car Park area.

THE OLD CAR PARK

The borders along the north-west face of the house are home to a number of plants of special value during the winter. The most imposing of these is *Garrya elliptica*; with its grey catkins this is an attractive subject at a dull time of year. To the right *Viburnum tinus* 'Eve Price' has pink-white flowers in clusters for a long season. For winter scent few plants are better than *Sarcococca confusa*, growing by the steps. The insignificant white flowers on this privet-like evergreen can be smelt from a distance on mild days.

West of the Old Car Park area is a selection of deciduous azaleas principally of the group known as Knap Hill Hybrids. These plants make a fine display in May, with flowers in a wide range of colours. The path through this area, known as Lock's Trail, has been recently planted with a selection of interesting trees and shrubs. A mature *Magnolia × soulangeana* can be seen immediately to the right, beyond which is a collection of New Zealand plants, including evergreen species of the southern beech, *Nothofagus*.

Heading south into the main garden along Lock's Trail is a woodland area rich with rhododendrons and camellias. Pacific Coast hybrid irises, a large group derived from species from the western seaboard of the U.S.A. and Canada, form an underplanting with evergreen leaves which make excellent ground-cover.

On the right side of the path is a plant of *Rhododendron argyrophyllum* spp. *nankingense*, from China. The large deep green leaves have a silvery white coating, known as indumentum, beneath. Pink bell-shaped flowers over 50mm (2in) across are born in large trusses in spring. Large-leafed rhododendrons make imposing foliage plants, and a number have been planted around the garden in recent years.

A tree of special note in this area is the rare *Ehretia dicksonii*, a tender small tree with bold leaves, which is prone to late frost damage. On the left hand side of the path are a number of fine flowering trees. The dogwood, *Cornus* 'Eddie's White Wonder', is a hybrid between two American species, with large white flowers in the spring. The white 'petals' are actually bracts, but serve the same purpose of attracting pollinators. Many dogwoods also give a fine display of autumn colour. In addition to dogwoods Rosemoor has a good collection of magnolias, including the Himalayan species *Magnolia campbellii*. The specimen here has some way to go before it will achieve its final height. The large pink flowers appear on leafless branches in early spring.

Amongst the herbaceous plants two species of the wood lily are of interest. Both come from North America. *Trillium grandiflorum*, the wake robin, has white flowers in spring, and is a fine plant for the woodland garden. *Trillium sessile* has purple flowers carried just above the mottled leaves.

The Primrose Bank, east of Rosemoor House

The path continues out towards the Main Lawn, alongside which is a fine specimen of *Betula ermanii*, with white bark. To the right the woodland theme continues with the glossy-leaved evergreen Californian bayberry, *Myrica californica*, a hardy shrub rarely seen in gardens. This is growing beneath a tree of *Magnolia sprengeri*, which has large deep pink flowers in early spring. A specimen of the purple Dawyck beech nearby makes a splash of colour amongst the greens of rhododendrons. To the rear of the bed, large bushes of *Rhododendron praevernum* bear bell-shaped pink-flushed white flowers in late winter and early spring.

A number of *Stewartia* species are planted in this area; with white or cream flowers in early summer, rich autumn colour, and attractive flaking bark, they have something to offer throughout the year.

A striking plant in late spring is the evergreen *Trochodendron aralioides*, a rare shrub of handsome habit with green flowers. A dogwood of note nearby is the hybrid *Cornus* 'Norman Hadden' (*C. kousa* × *nuttallii*), grown from a plant propagated from the original specimen.

Continuing towards the end of the bed amongst a number of interesting shrubs are the Tasmanian *Eucryphia milliganii*, with a profusion of small white flowers in summer, and *Parrotia persica* 'Pendula', the latter striking in its autumn colour effect. Flanking the entrance to the garden from the Old Car Park is a fine variegated holly, *Ilex aquifolium* 'Handsworth New Silver' alongside which the winter-flowering *Mahonia japonica* shelters at its base the spring-flowering *Cyclamen repandum* with its fragrant, reddish purple flowers.

ROSEMOOR HOUSE

The beds along the front and side of the house contain many tender subjects, enjoying the south-westerly aspect. The balcony provides support for the climbing rose 'Handel' with large creamy white flowers, pink-flushed as they age. A fine scented shrub in the border is *Viburnum carlesii* 'Diana', whose flowers open red and fade to white. Further along the border *Olearia (Pachystegia) insignis*, from New Zealand, bears large white daisy flower-heads over its rhododendron-like leaves in summer.

On the house itself and to the left of the door grows *Rosa banksiae* 'Lutea', with a large *Wisteria sinensis* to the right. The old conservatory area has several interesting climbers: *Robinia hispida*, with deep rose-pink flowers, and the strong-growing *Wisteria venusta* 'Violacea' with its large purple flowers.

The front of Rosemoor House, where many tender plants grow well in this sheltered position

Among the herbaceous plants the yellow iris-like *Moraea spathulata* is a rarity. Several troughs in this area contain a number of interesting dwarf and alpine plants.

The path to the left leads to a fine specimen of *Prunus serrula*, whose rich mahogany-hued bark is a particularly striking feature. Directly across the path a gravel area contains the columnar *Juniperus drupacea*, with purple and green-leafed phormiums providing an effective foliage contrast.

On the left-hand side of the path a mixed planting contains a *Roscoea* species, *R. purpurea*, whose purple orchid-like flowers are a striking sight in early summer. The elegant *Dierama pulcherrimum* bears long wands of hanging flowers from mid summer onwards, ranging in colour from white through to deep purple. A number of small trees here are of interest. *Pinus mugo*, from central Europe, has slowly reached 5m (16½ft) high. Further along, a sycamore cultivar, *Acer pseudoplatanus* 'Brilliantissimum' provides a colourful foliage effect, pink in spring, ageing slowly through cream to yellow-green. Beneath it grows the yellow dog's tooth violet, *Erythronium* 'Pagoda'.

In the bed across the path from the *Prunus serrula* a number of winter-flowering subjects have been planted, with herbaceous plants and shrubs along the path to prolong the season of display, particularly by coloured or bold foliage. Notable plants in this bed include *Cornus controversa* with its tiered habit, reaching nearly 6m (20ft), and *Magnolia kobus*, from Japan, planted in 1966. Beneath it and along the edge of the bed is a selection of viburnums and philadelphus.

17

THE OLD KITCHEN GARDEN

In the bed across the path the Chilean shrub *Sophora macrocarpa* bears its yellow pea flowers in early spring. The wall opposite, facing due south-west, is home to a number of tender and unusual plants. Using bold-leafed subjects such as *Cordyline, Phormium*, hardy palms (*Trachycarpus*), and the loquat (*Eriobotrya*), the effect of a 'sub-tropical' planting is obtained, with plants which are hardy over much of the country, joined in summer by tender plants such as *Musa basjoo* (the banana palm) and hedychium species (ginger lilies).

Along the wall behind a selection of climbing or wall shrubs grows, including the summer-flowering pineapple-scented *Cytisus battandieri*, and *Trachelospermum jasminoides*, the latter an attractive evergreen climber with scented white flowers. Early flowers are obtained from *Clematis cirrhosa* var. *balearica*, in January in a mild season.

Moving into the Cherry Garden there are some very large rambling roses such as *Rosa* 'Bobbie James' and 'Paul's Himalayan Musk' in the flowering cherry trees to the west. A large plant of the pampas grass, *Cortaderia argentea* 'Sunningdale Silver', bears its 2.5m (8ft) high plumes in autumn. Of special note in the border is a handsome evergreen *Viburnum*, *V. cylindricum* from China, whose leaves grow up to 200 mm (8in) long. *Betula medwedewii* nearby has a strongly ascendant branch habit. At the end of the bed are a number of hydrangeas, including *Hydrangea aspera* from West China, a fine summer-flowering species. This area is richly underplanted with choice woodland subjects such as *Trillium, Tricyrtis, Dactylorhiza* and *Helleborus*.

Backing the shrub bed is a mixed beech and holly hedge, with two large tulip trees (*Liriodendron tulipifera*) beyond, planted in 1932. To the right the coral bark maple, *Acer palmatum* 'Senkaki', has attractive pink-red stems in the winter. Beneath it grows *Berberis hypokerina*, with handsome large holly-like evergreen leaves. A mixture of cyclamen, snowdrops, crocuses, native orchids and *Narcissus* species gives a long season of display beneath the tulip trees.

Along the path leading from the Stone Garden to the house are azaleas, *Ilex crenata* and *Magnolia* 'Leonard Messel' (left)

The path then moves south-east towards the Stone Garden. To the right numerous species and cultivars of hellebore provide excellent late winter colour, ranging from pure white and green through rose to deep purple. Lenten roses, *Helleborus orientalis* forms, provide the main display here, with the deep purple *H. atrorubens* amongst the earliest to flower. This planting also includes the native green-flowered *H. foetidus*, and the imposing *H. argutifolius*.

On the left *Erica carnea* 'Springwood White' grows with a number of azaleas and rhododendrons. Nearby *Prunus* 'Kursar', a hybrid raised by Collingwood Ingram, bears a multitude of small rich pink flowers in early spring. The next major feature is the area known as the Stone Garden.

18 19

STONE AND WOODLAND GARDENS

To the east of the Stone Garden numerous camellias brighten the early spring season. One of the most valuable of these is the hybrid *Camellia* × *williamsii* 'St Ewe', with single pink flowers borne over a long season.

Woodland Garden Immediately due east a gate leads to a track, from which a small flight of steps leads into the Woodland Garden, created on the steep west-facing slope. This area is planted principally with ericaceous plants, and is most

Prunus incisa, camellias and heathers of late March in the Woodland Garden

attractive in springtime when azaleas and rhododendrons are in full flower. A wide range of other woodland plants in genera such as *Pieris, Camellia* and *Vaccinium*, as well as numerous flowering trees, provide extra seasonal interest. All greatly appreciate the shelter provided by the canopy of oak trees.

The Stone Garden, where slow-growing conifers provide year-round effect. With the architectural influence of the lion and stonework, this garden is evocative of times past

At the top of the steps, immediately to the right is a plant of the climbing *Hydrangea petiolaris*, growing up a young oak, much as this species might do in its natural habitat. Bearing left along the path parallel to the track, to the left is a plant of the handsome large-leafed Canary Island holly, *Ilex platyphylla*. A number of flowering cherries are planted in this area, including *Prunus incisa*, grown from a sucker from an original introduction by Collingwood Ingram, renowned for his work to popularise cherries.

After making a sharp right turn at the end of the path an interesting tender pine from Mexico can be seen, *Pinus montezumae*, with long glaucous needles, planted in 1962. Nearby, plants of *Eucryphia* 'Nymansay' of the same vintage give a fine display of white flowers in mid to late summer.

Stone Garden After following the track due south, the path leading back to the Stone Garden through the wrought-

27

iron gates is to the right. Here a number of ferns flourish in the damp shade, and also growing in this area is a fine plant of the rare Moutan peony, *Paeonia suffruticosa* 'Rock's Variety', which has large white flowers in late spring, each petal bearing a deep maroon blotch. A strong architectural element is given by the contrasting form of upright junipers and conical dwarf conifers such as *Picea albertiana* 'Conica' and *Thuja occidentalis* 'Rheingold', with the low growing hummocks of the purple-leafed Japanese maple, *Acer palmatum* 'Dissectum Atropurpureum', on either side of the path to the right. *Taxus baccata* 'Standishii' to the left of these is another fine year-round feature, with its erect habit and golden foliage.

Thuja 'Rheingold' (left), *Juniperus communis* 'Hibernica' and *J. scopulorum* 'Skyrocket' in the Stone Garden

THE MAIN DRIVE

To reach the Main Drive, take the path immediately due west of the Stone Garden, bordered by a high hedge of *Chamaecyparis pisifera* 'Squarrosa' to the left. Several clones of *Mahonia* × *media* on the right show the variation in this valuable late autumn-flowering hybrid. A fine spring-flowering *Berberis, B. valdiviana*, combines glossy evergreen foliage and saffron-coloured flowers in early spring.

In the centre of the grass area leading towards the Main Drive is a tree of *Pyrus calleryana* 'Chanticleer', of upright habit, and early flowering. To the left is a fine flowering cherry, *Prunus* 'Taoyama Zakura', planted in 1961. Herbaceous plants in this bed include the rare *Lobelia laxiflora* var. *angustifolia*, with narrow tubular red and yellow flowers borne over a long season.

THE OLD TENNIS COURT

Turning left the steps lead up to the Old Tennis Court area. The initial plantings here were made in 1979 and the whole area was revised and replanted in 1994, with further improvements being made annually as these fast-growing plants are often short-lived. This area is home to a selection of plants from Mediterranean climates such as California, New Zealand, Australia, South Africa and of course the Mediterranean itself. There are good representations of genera such as *Cistus, Ozothamnus, Cytisus* and many plants with silver and aromatic foliage, such as *Artemisia*, grown here to take advantage of the more sheltered, sunny location, in raised beds which have been specially prepared by incorporating large quantities of grit to improve their drainage.

In the south-east corner of the Tennis Court is a large specimen of *Eucalyptus glaucescens* (Tingirini Gum), with attractive bark which peels off in long strips, and distinctive sickle-shaped leaves. The bank on which this tree stands contains many hardy New Zealand plants.

THE CROQUET LAWN

From the north-east corner of the Tennis Court steps lead you uphill and onto the Croquet Lawn through an area of ericaceous and associated plants which form a link with the Stone Garden. In 1996 the main bank of the Croquet Lawn area, just below and in the shelter of the Woodland Garden, was refurbished. The microclimate here allows us to grow many unusual evergreens and southern hemisphere plants, including South American and Tasmanian subjects. Some particularly striking Chilean plants grow on this bank, including *Embothrium coccineum* (the Chilean firebush) with its vivid orange-scarlet flowers, several *Azara* which bear vanilla-scented, mimosa-like flowers in late winter, and *Crinodendron*. Also to be found with this group of plants is the distinctive New Zealand evergreen *Pittosporum dallii*.

THE ARBORETUM

Following the path down towards the Old Tennis Court, the entrance to the Arboretum is to the left, flanked by two examples of the variegated cherry laurel, *Prunus laurocerasus* 'Variegata'.

The Arboretum plantings include many interesting and rare trees and shrubs planted by Lady Anne Berry, and extend along to the valley of the spring which once marked the previous southern boundary of the garden.

Planting began in 1975, pre-dated by the fine mature walnut tree (*Juglans regia*) which dominates the area, and from which various rides radiate. A wide range of genera is planted here, with many specimens frequently grown from wild-source seed. The genera well represented include *Quercus* (oaks), *Sorbus, Nothofagus* (southern beech), *Carya* (hickory), *Zelkova, Pterocarya* (wingnut), maples, birches, and various conifers. Plantings in the Arboretum are deliberately close, with a view to thinning-out as the trees grow.

Immediately to the left of the Arboretum entrance a planting of small trees and shrubs provides rapid interest and colour as the larger trees between them mature. Silver and yellow predominate, the former from *Pyrus salicifolia* 'Pendula' and *P. nivalis*, with *Acer japonicum* 'Aureum', *Lonicera nitida* 'Baggesen's Gold' and *Pinus sylvestris* 'Aureus' supplying the yellow interest as their names suggest; the latter is especially effective in winter.

A number of shrub roses also grow in this area, many chosen for fruit as well as flower. A good example is *Rosa moyesii*, which bears single flowers from deep pink to red, and has attractive flagon-shaped hips in autumn.

The South Arboretum

At the end of Lady Anne's Arboretum a broad grass causeway leads into the triangular field beyond, where the South Arboretum is being developed. Bog and marginal plantings above and below the causeway continue the theme of plantings along the stream to the west of the Underpass. This field has the best natural drainage and finest soil of the entire Rosemoor estate, and is being developed as an informal area with broad tree and shrub plantings around the perimeter, and parkland specimens in grass within.

The Underpass which carries the path back to the visitors centre lies to the west of the entrance to the South Arboretum.

CONCLUSION

The initial development of Rosemoor as a truly national garden will take ten years. During that time the major features already described will mature, and others as yet only in the initial planning stage will be developed. However, many years will pass before the garden will be truly mature. Therein lies the distinctive appeal and excitement of Rosemoor, in that visitors and RHS members will be able to witness this process taking place, as a national garden rises from the fields of the Rosemoor estate.

But that is by no means the whole story, for alongside the development of the garden at Rosemoor, the Society has also created a Regional Centre for the RHS, to serve the West Country. Many activities of interest to gardeners and garden lovers already take place, centred upon Rosemoor and Cannington College in Bridgewater, Somerset. RHS members may attend garden walks, demonstrations, workshops and lectures, all of which have proved extremely popular. Advice on garden problems is also available from Rosemoor.

Rosemoor has much to offer the visitor, with the combination of Lady Anne's Garden, the new garden, and the Robin Herbert Centre, with its fine facilities. As each phase of development is completed there is yet more to see, a wider range of styles and plantings. Alongside this is the fascination of noting how the various parts of the garden mature. Rosemoor Garden is a garden to visit again and again, and there is no better way to keep in touch with developments at Rosemoor, than by becoming a member of The Royal Horticultural Society.

Many parts of Rosemoor are accessible by wheelchair

CREDITS

Written by Christopher
Bailes

Map of garden by Gail
Rose & John Fitzmaurice

Map on back cover by
Neil Chapman

Designed by Gail Rose &
John Fitzmaurice

Typeset by SX
Composing DTP,
Rayleigh, Essex

Printed by The KPC
Group, London and
Ashford, Kent

Photographs: RHS,
Rosemoor with the
exception of the
following:
C. P. Bailes pp. 4, 17;
Andrew Lawson pp. 1,
3, 18, 20, 22, 25, 26;
Derek St. Romaine front
cover, pp. 4-5, 13, 14, 23;
C. J. Rougier pp. 11, 15.

RHS GARDEN ROSEMOOR

Masterplan landscape
architects:
Elizabeth Banks
Associates

The Robin Herbert
Centre architect:
David Caird of Ferguson
Mann

ROSEMOOR THROUGH THE SEASONS

Each season has much to offer, from spring's welcome bloom, summer's dramatic profusion of colour and growth and the tangy scents and brilliance of autumn, to the winter months, a perfect time for quiet walks, to listen for bird song and look for animal tracks. Below are a few, among many, areas to note.

SPRING

Lakeside meadow of *Narcissus cyclamineus* and *N. bulbocodium*
Lady Anne's Garden rhododendrons, azaleas, magnolias, hellebores, daffodils
Formal Gardens Japanese cherries
Cottage Garden bulbs
Stream and Bog Gardens *Gunnera*, marsh marigolds, irises
Visitors centre area spring bedding

SUMMER

Formal Gardens shrub and modern roses; Spiral Garden (soft colours); Square Garden (hot colours)
Long Border plume poppies, lilies, campanulas, anemones
Visitors centre area tender perennials (July-October)
Potager, Herb Garden and **Cottage Garden**
Stream Garden irises, astilbes, polygonums

AUTUMN

Lady Anne's Garden autumn colour in the Arboretum; fruits and berries
Lakeside autumn colours reflected in the water
Formal Gardens late-flowering perennials, penstemons, chrysanthemums

WINTER

Arboretum evergreens and tree shapes
Lakeside winter colour of barks and stems
Lady Anne's Garden camellias (February), evergreens